HALLOWEEN COLORING BOOK

Halloween Coloring Book

Copyrights © T K Setzer

All Right Reserved

ISBN: 9781728648392

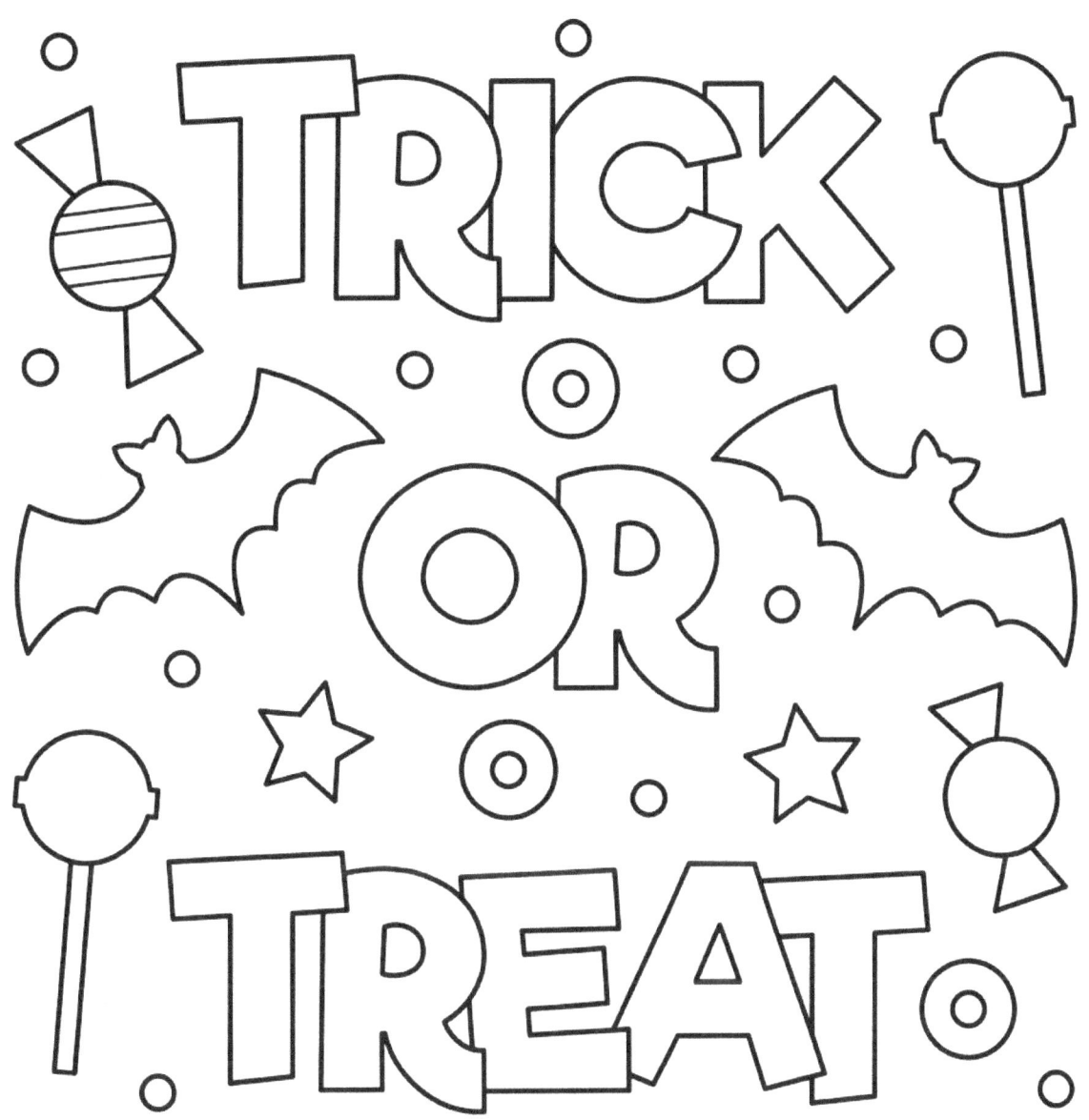

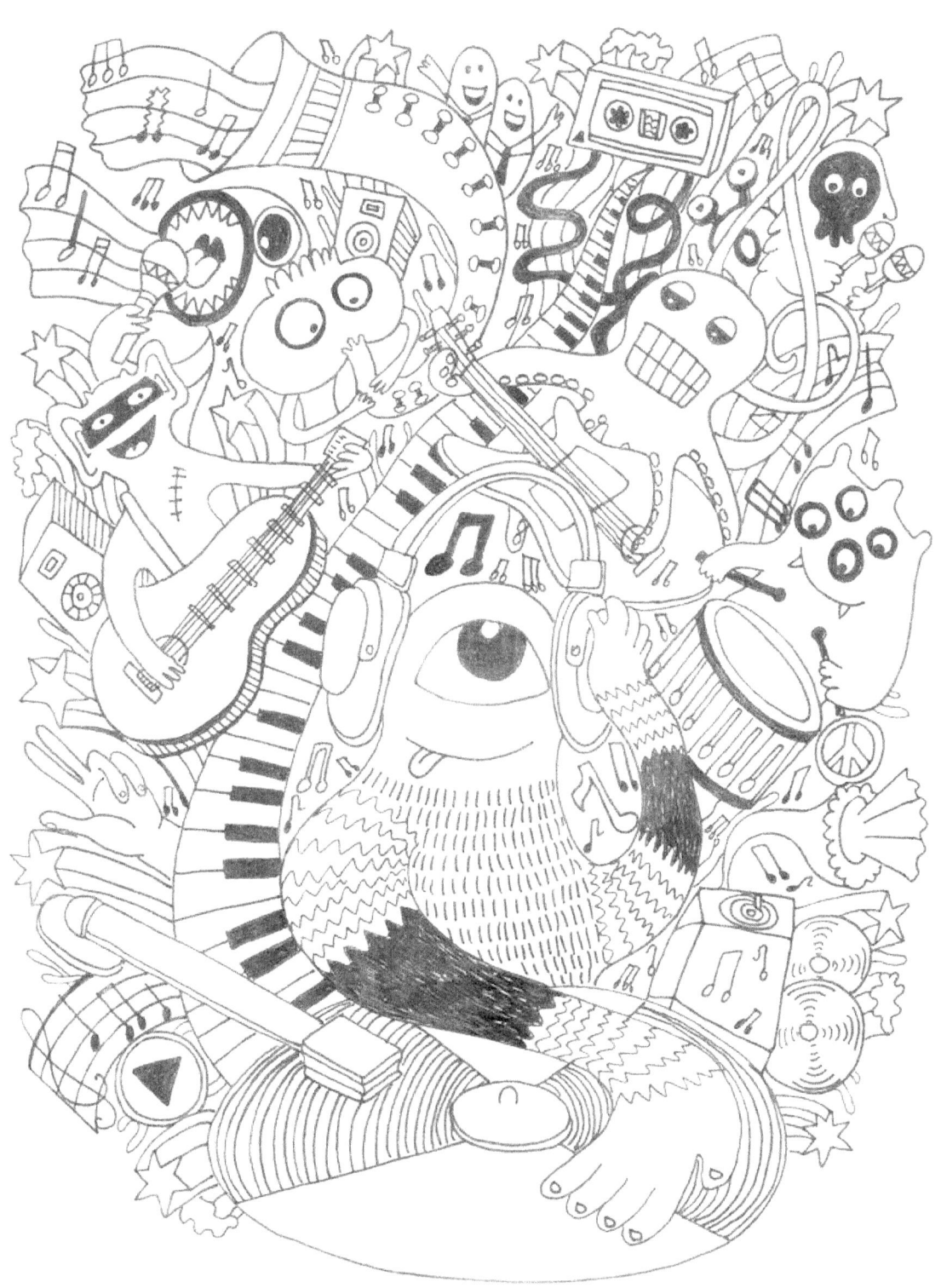

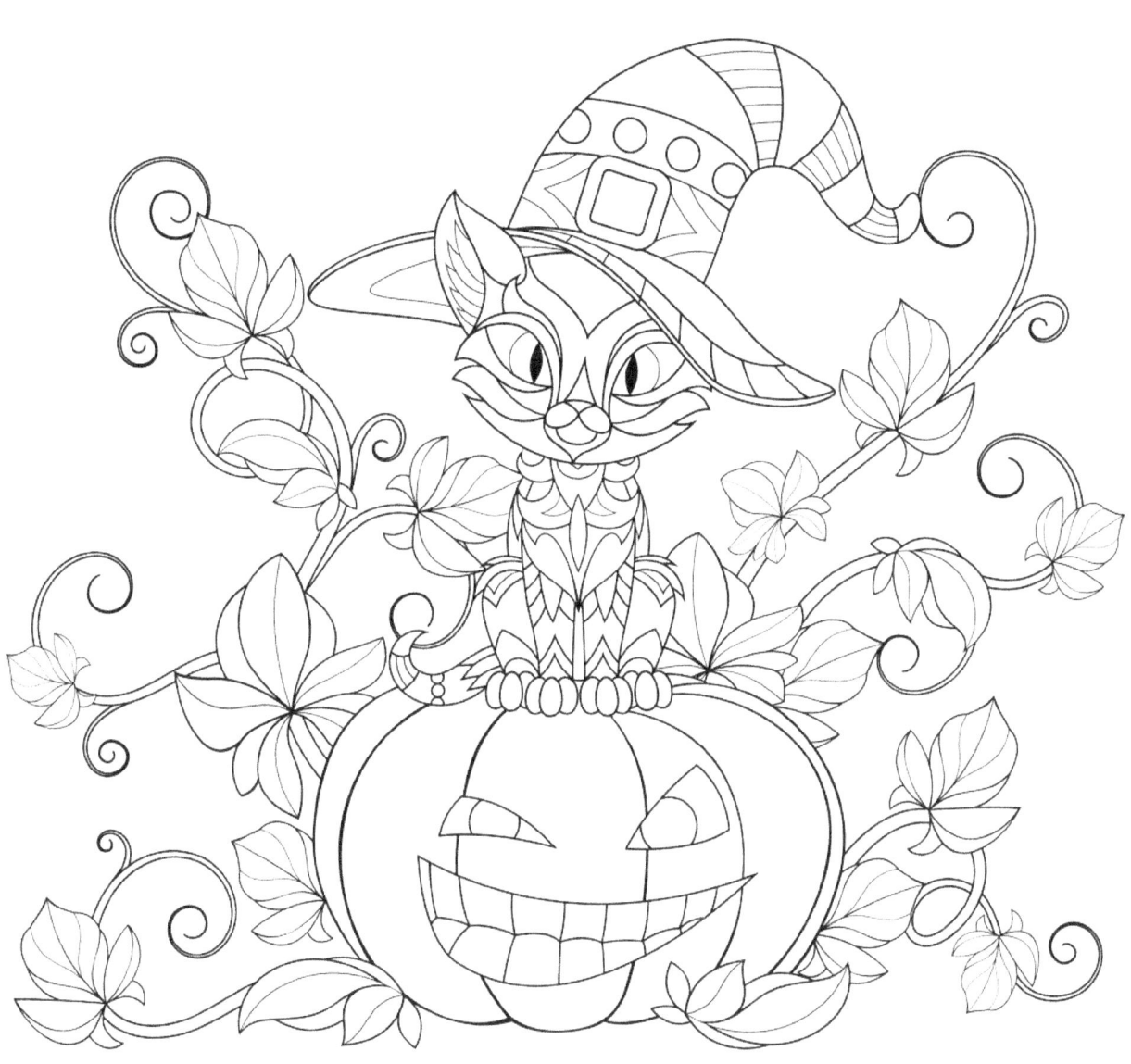

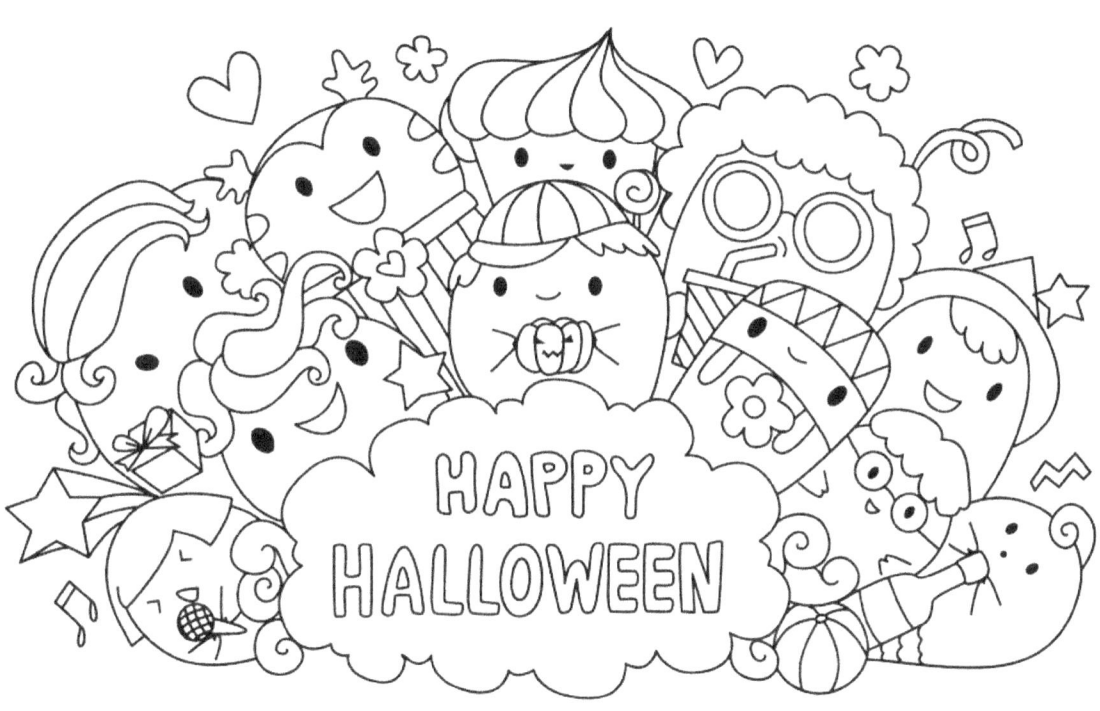

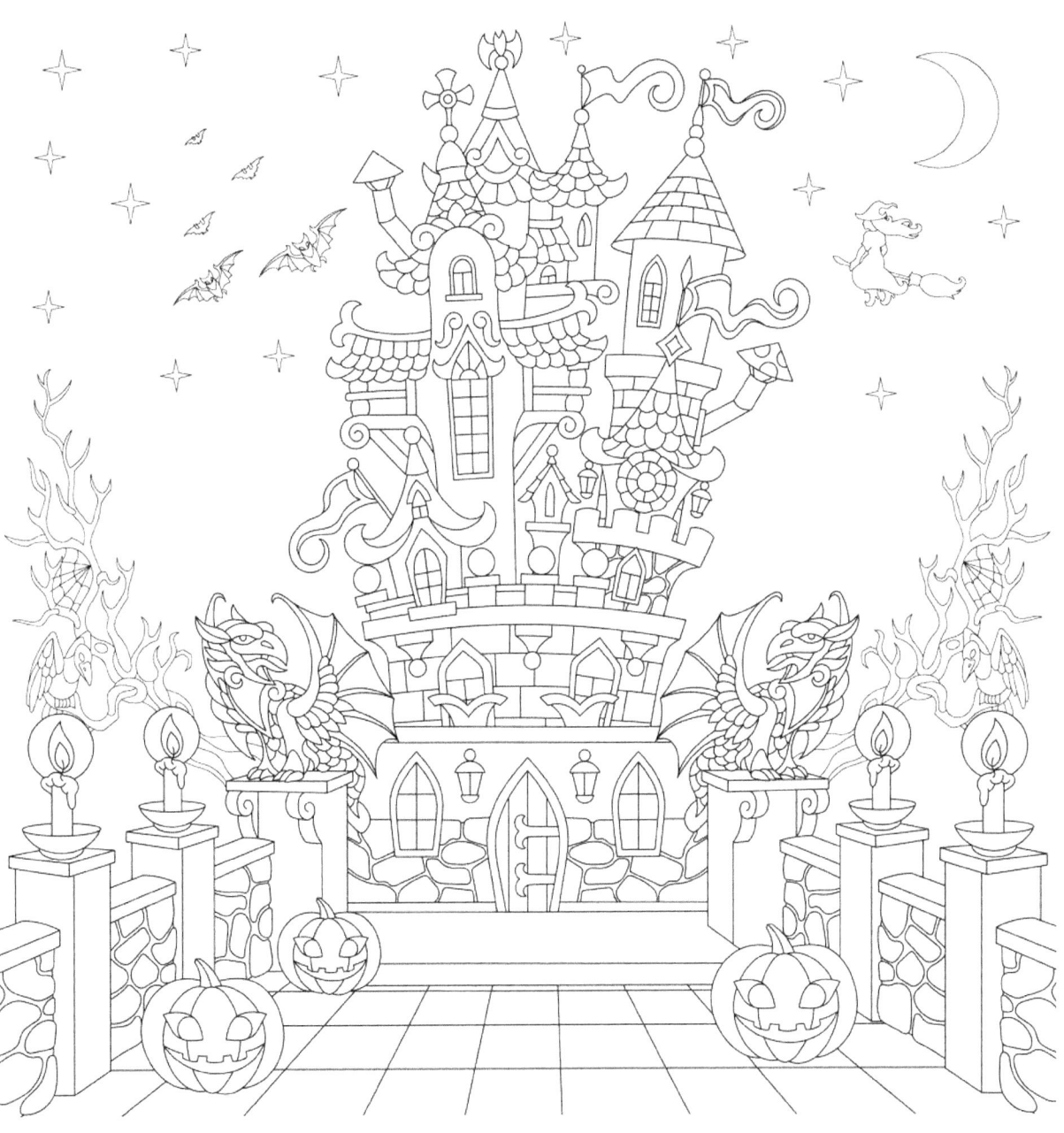

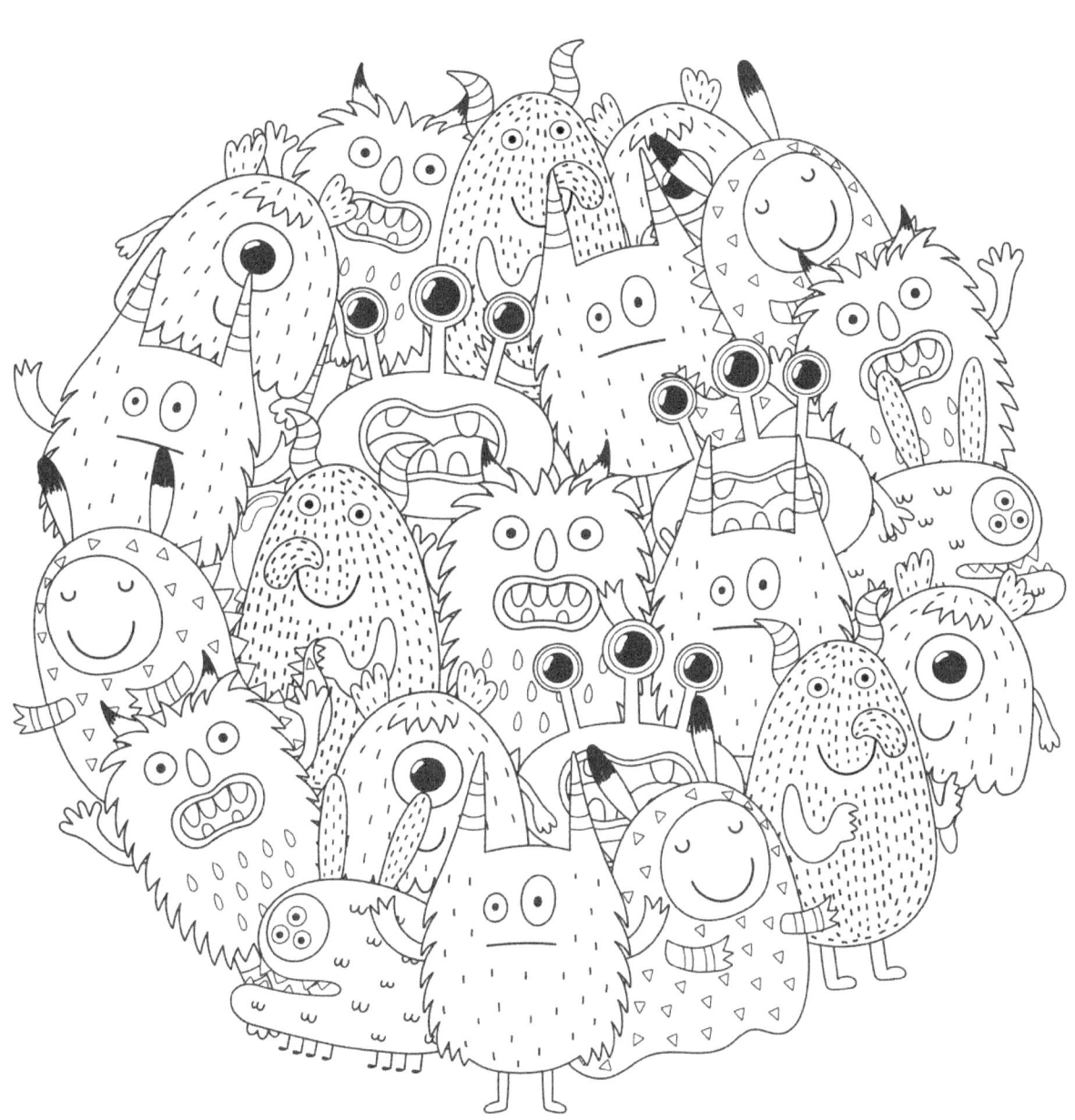

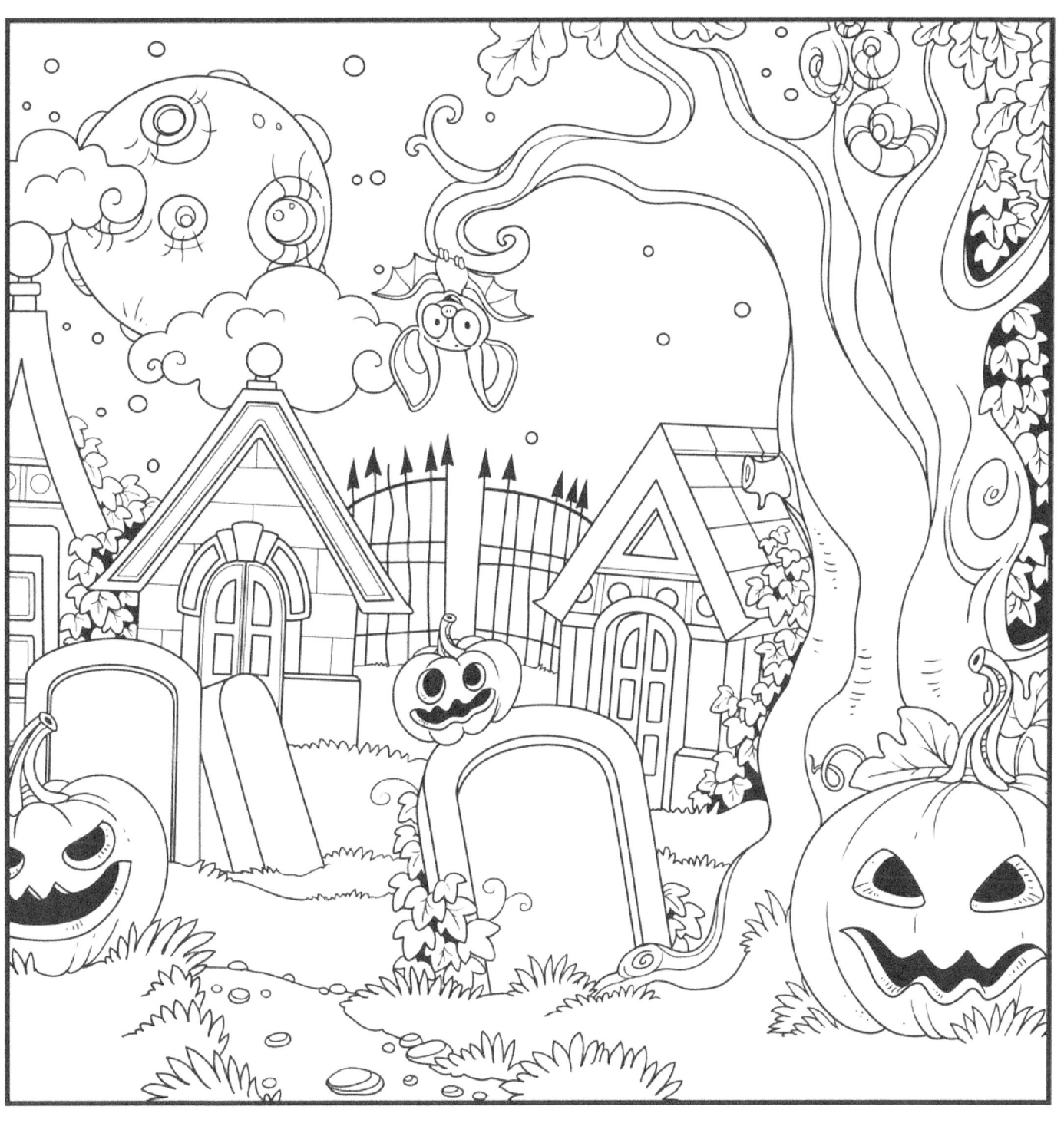

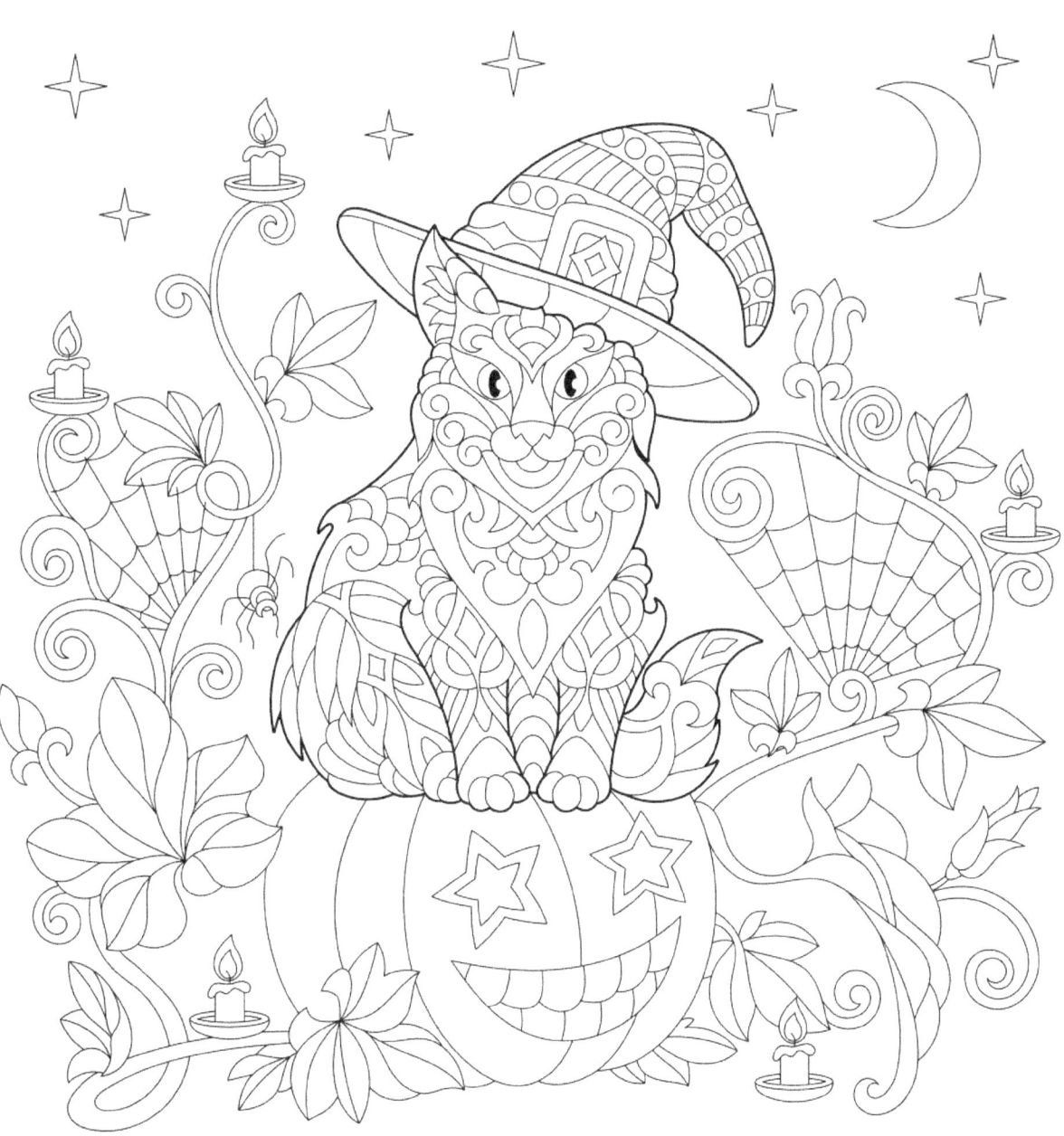

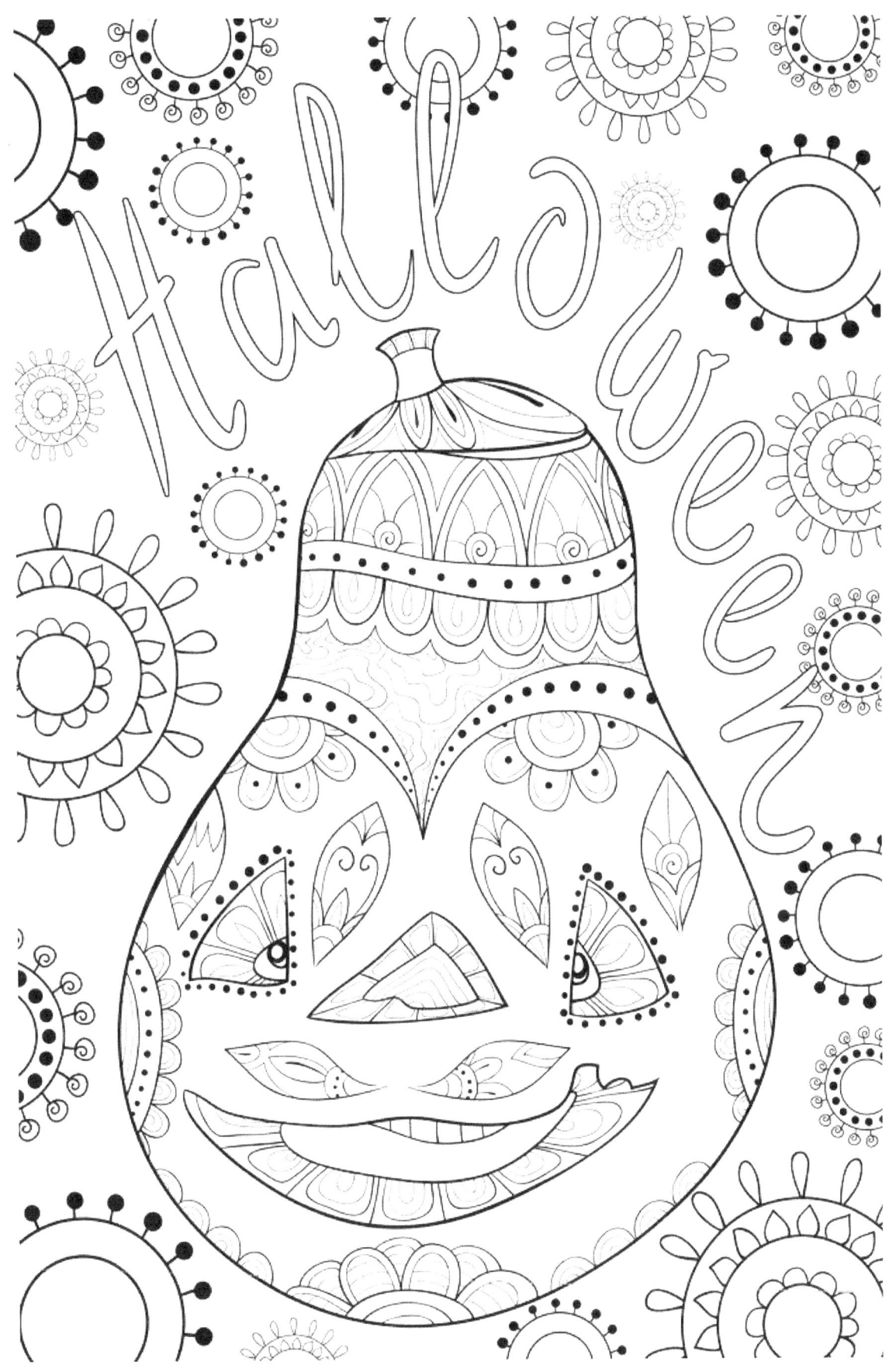

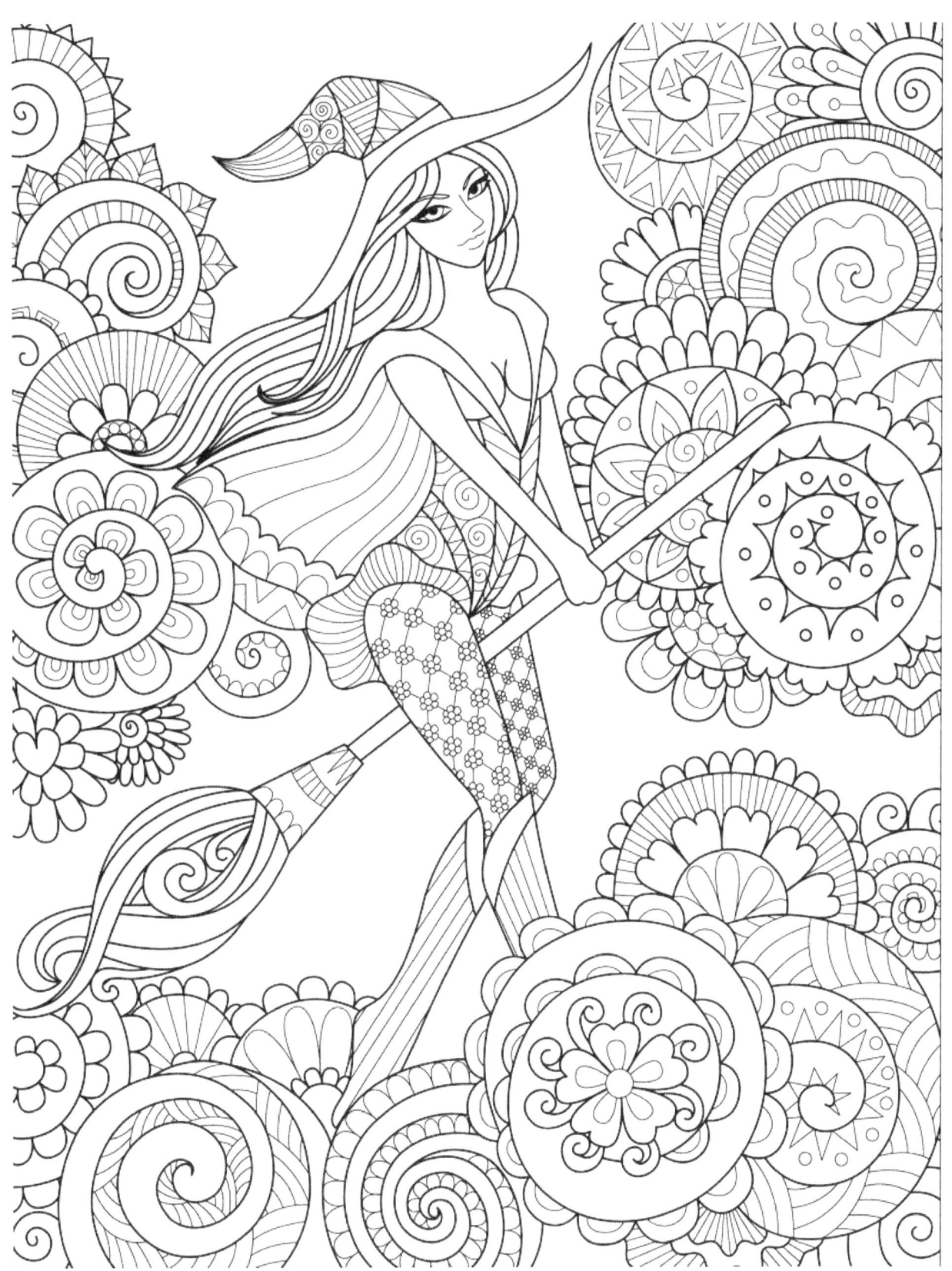

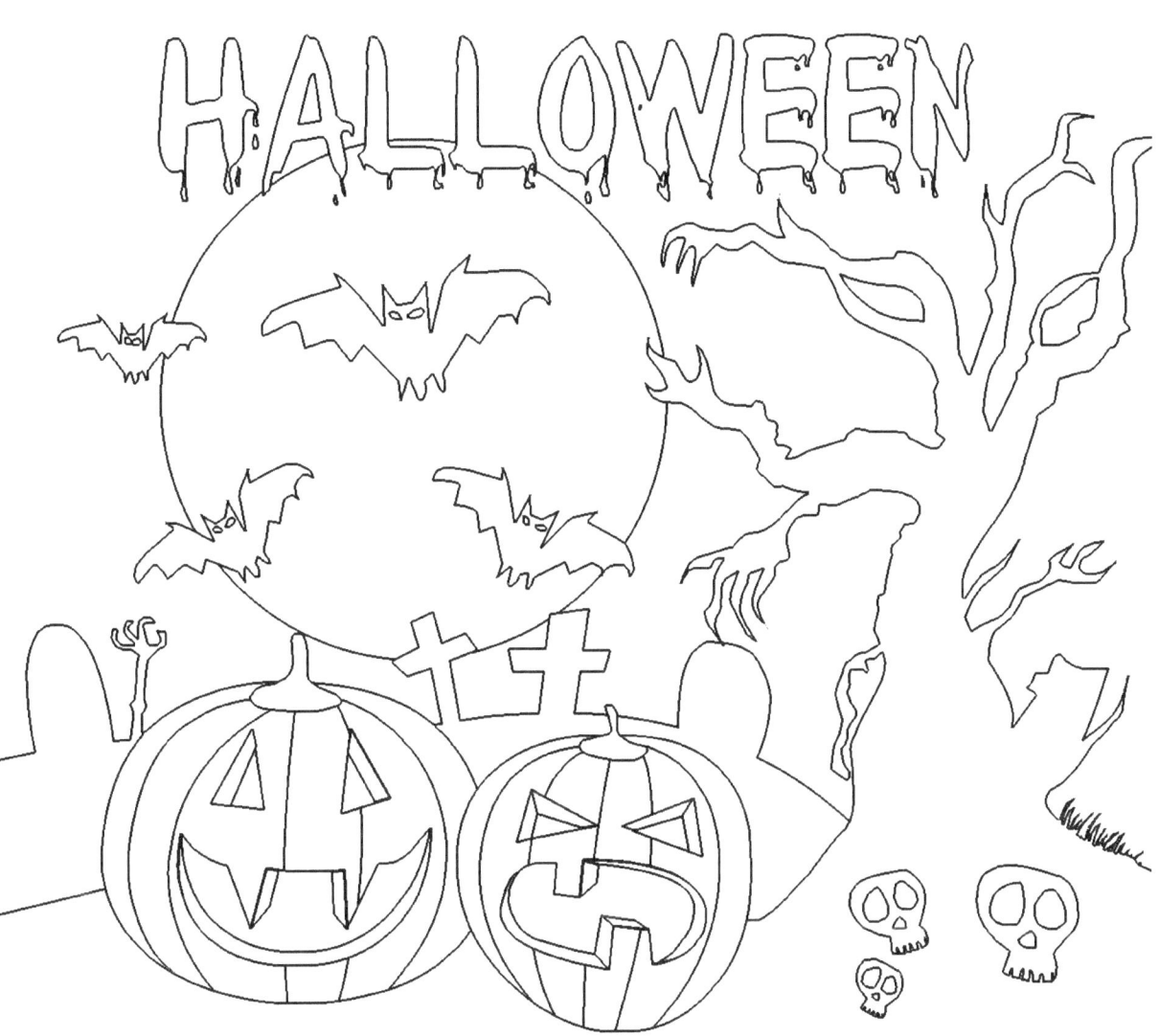

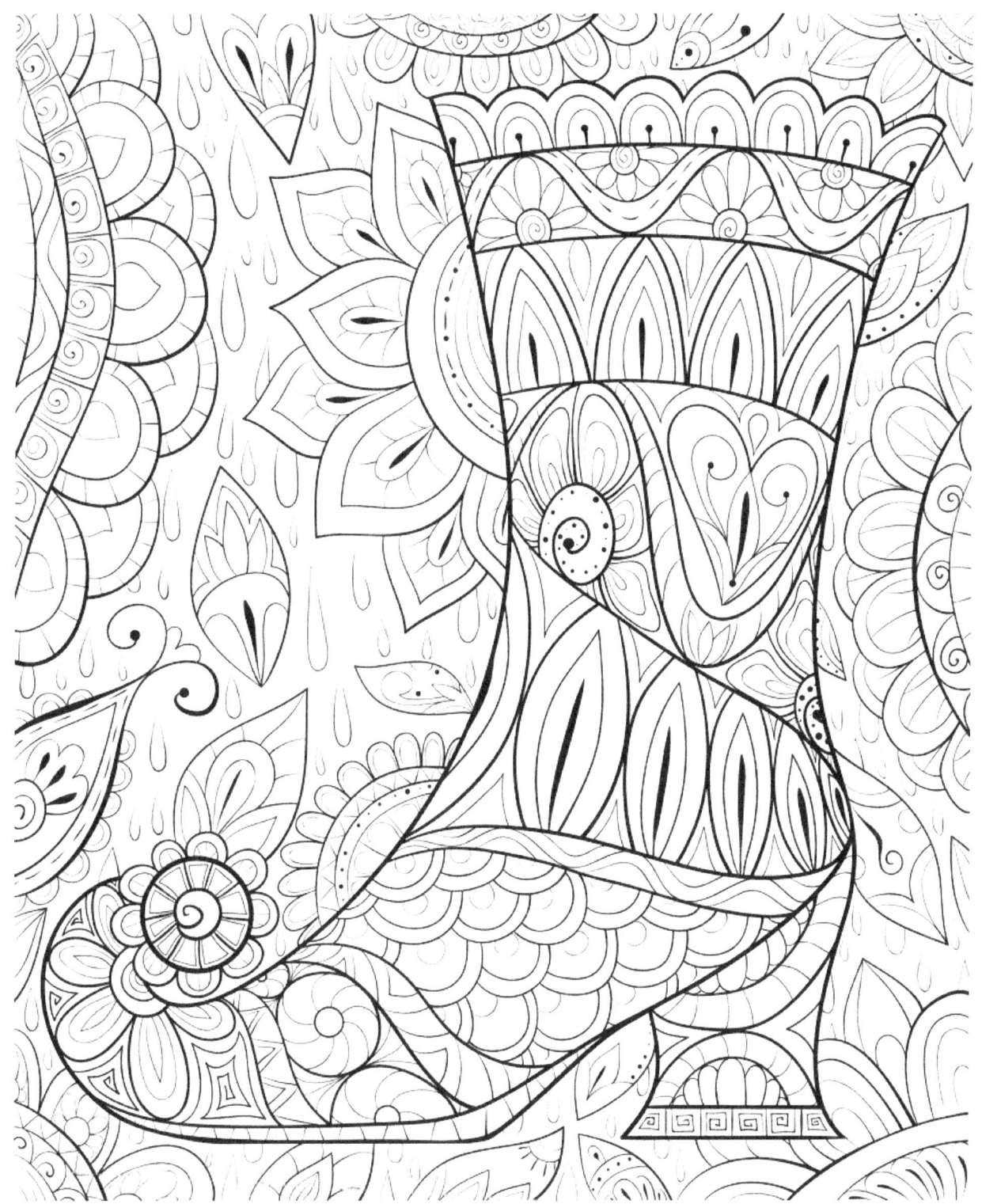

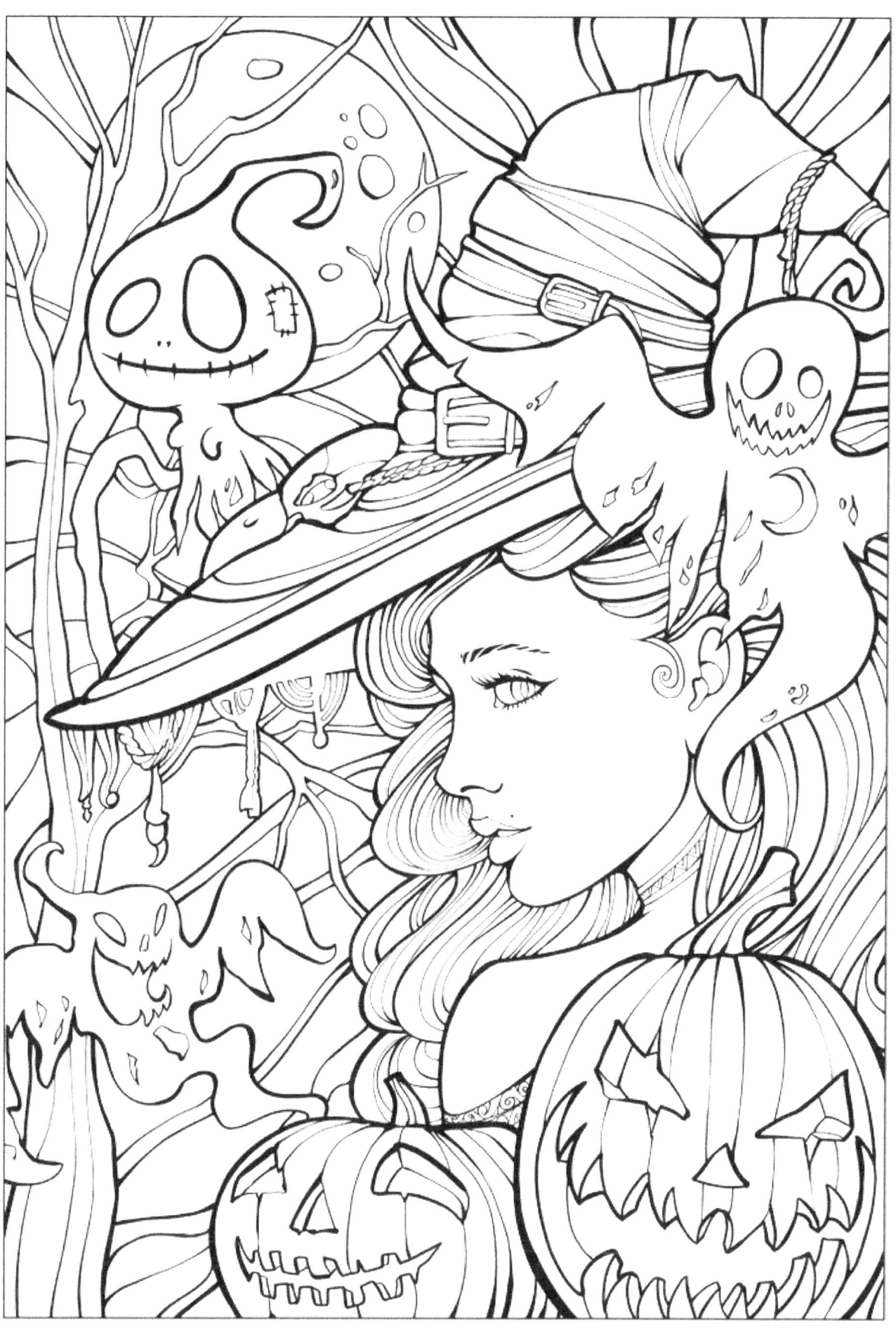

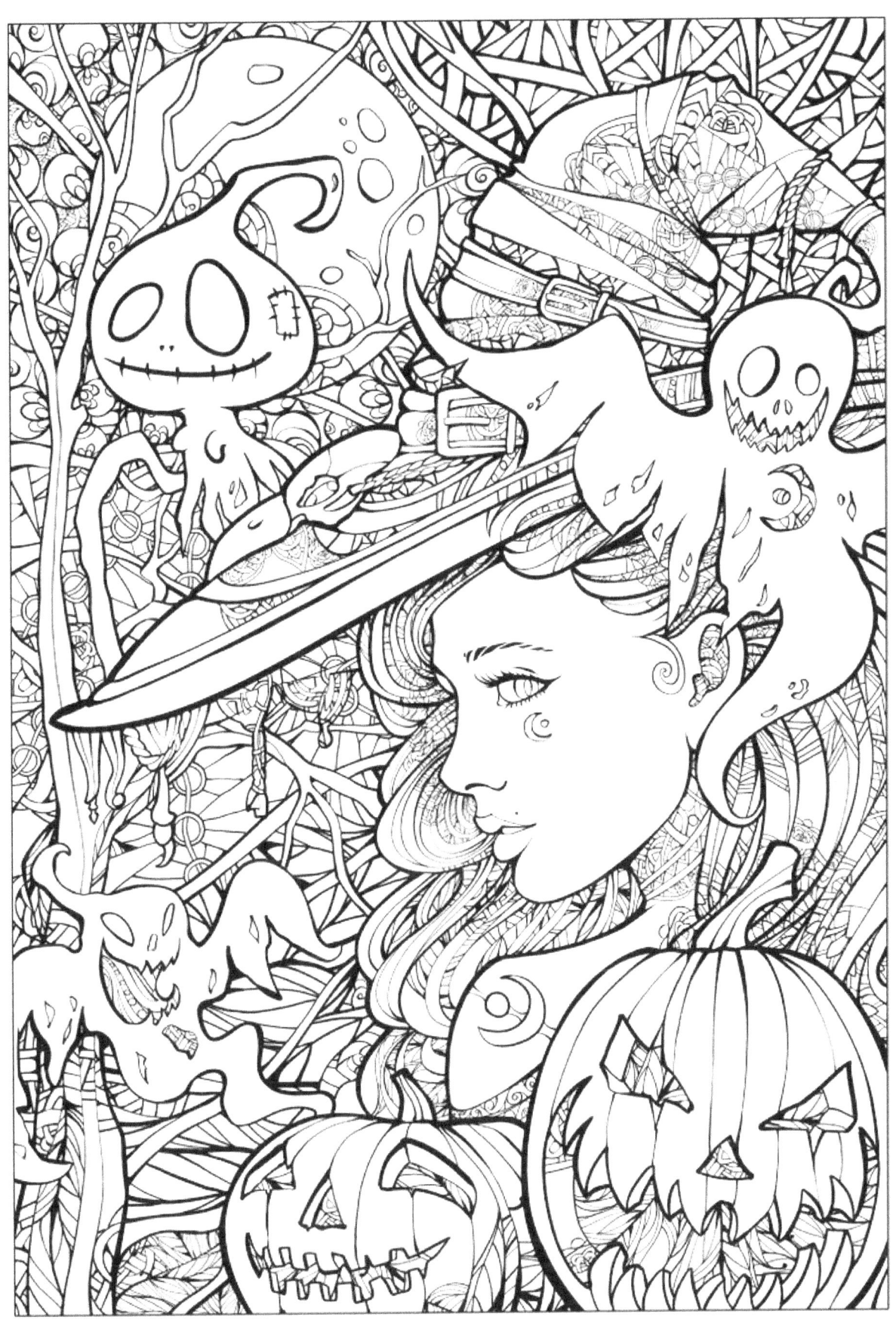

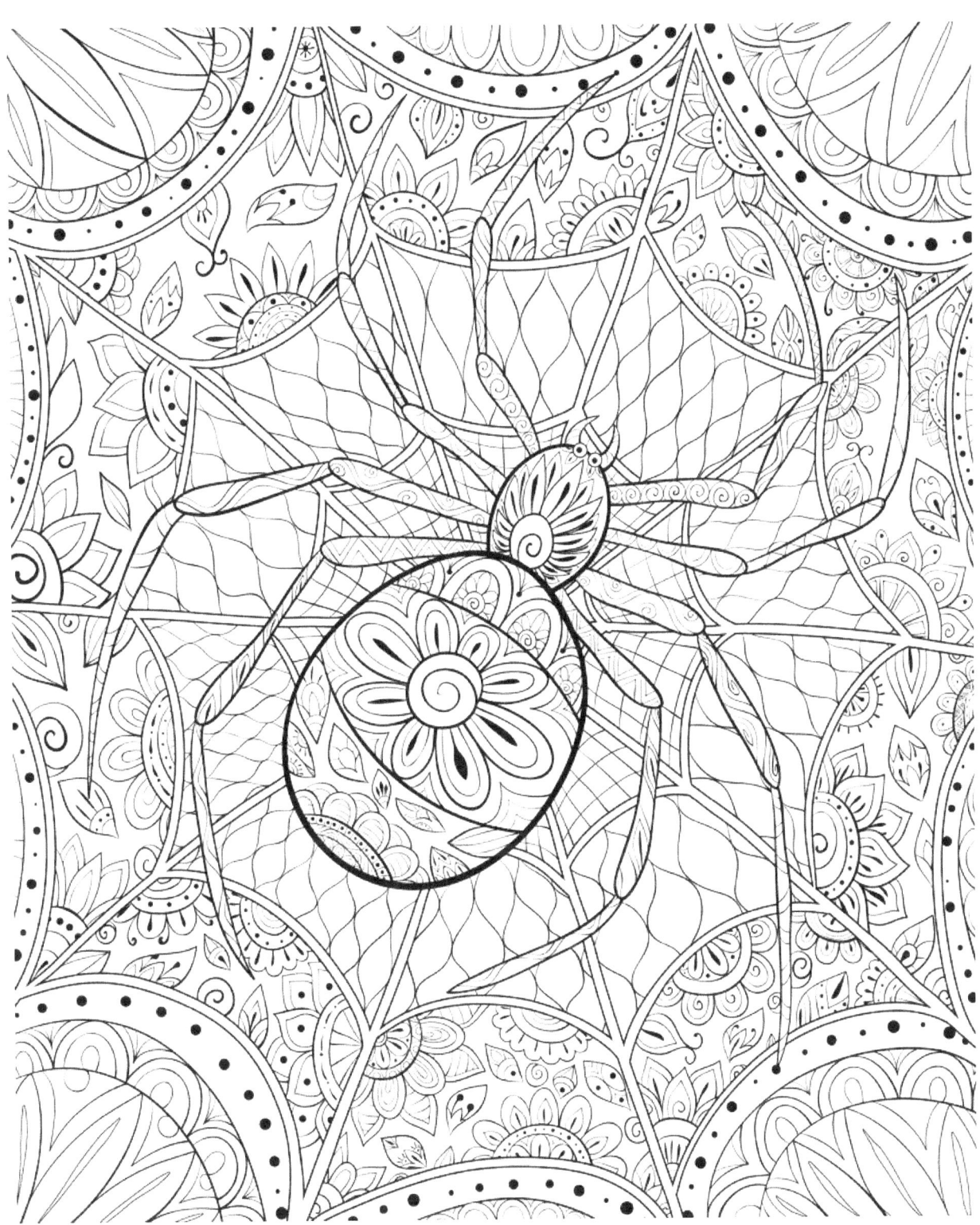

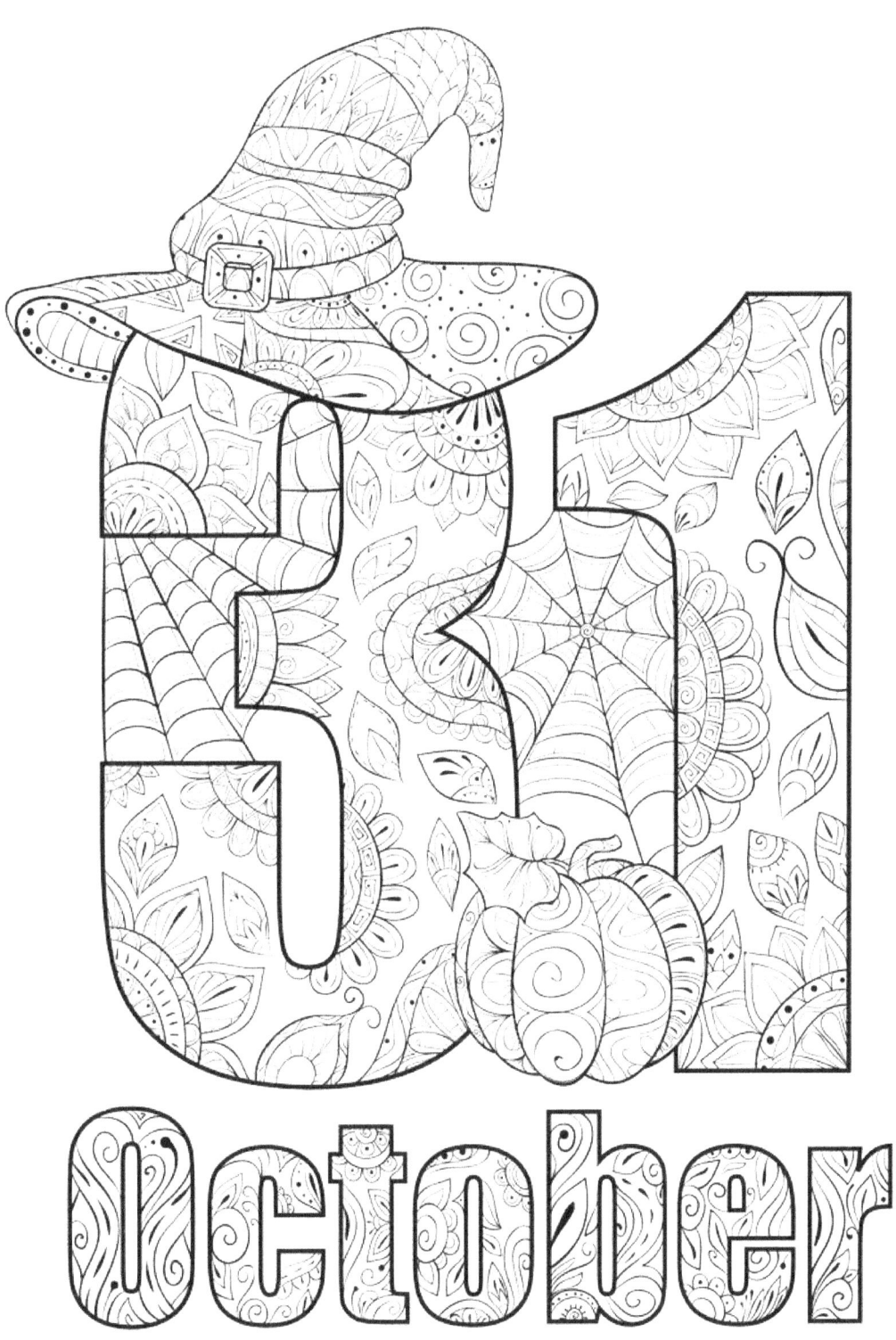

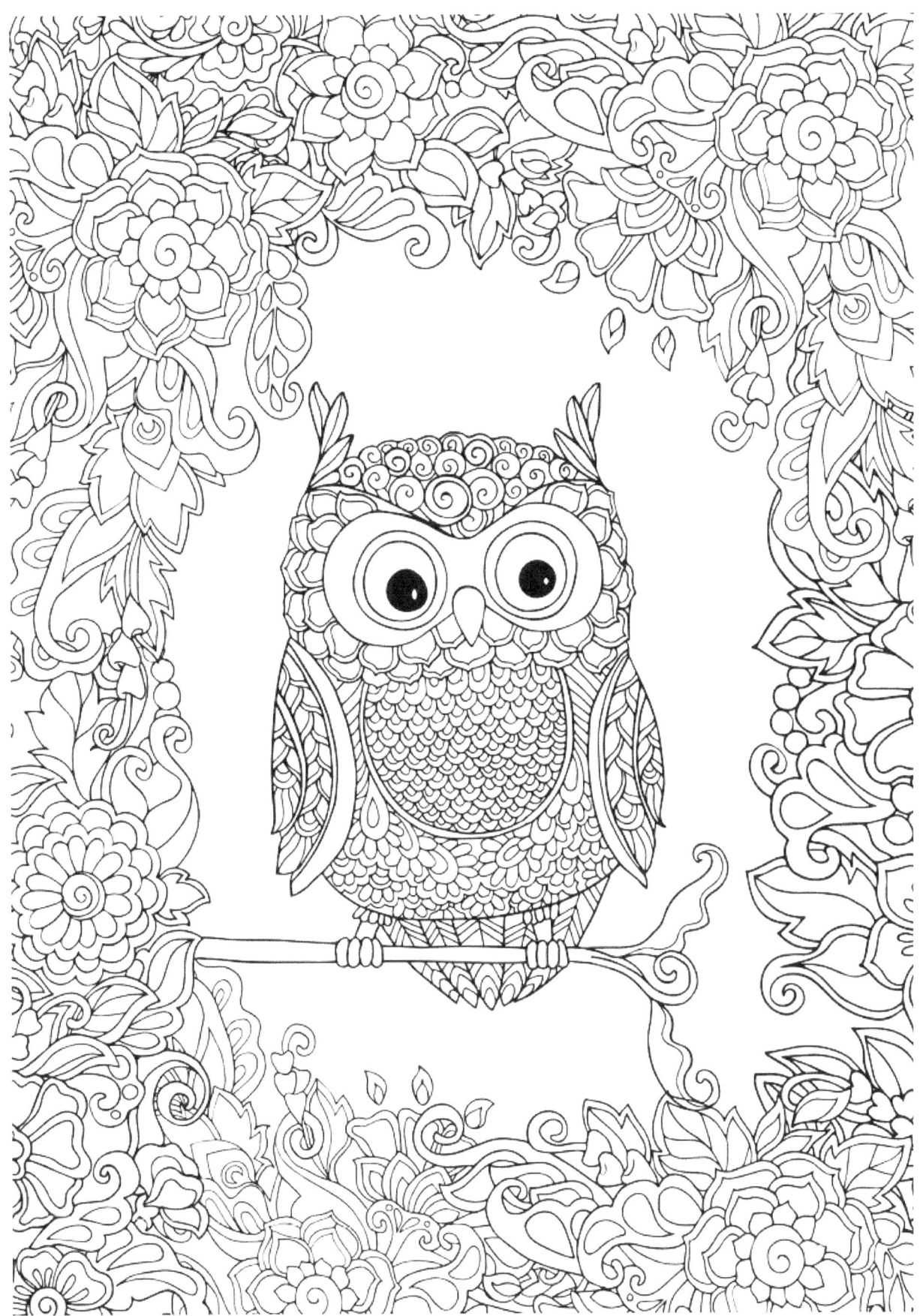

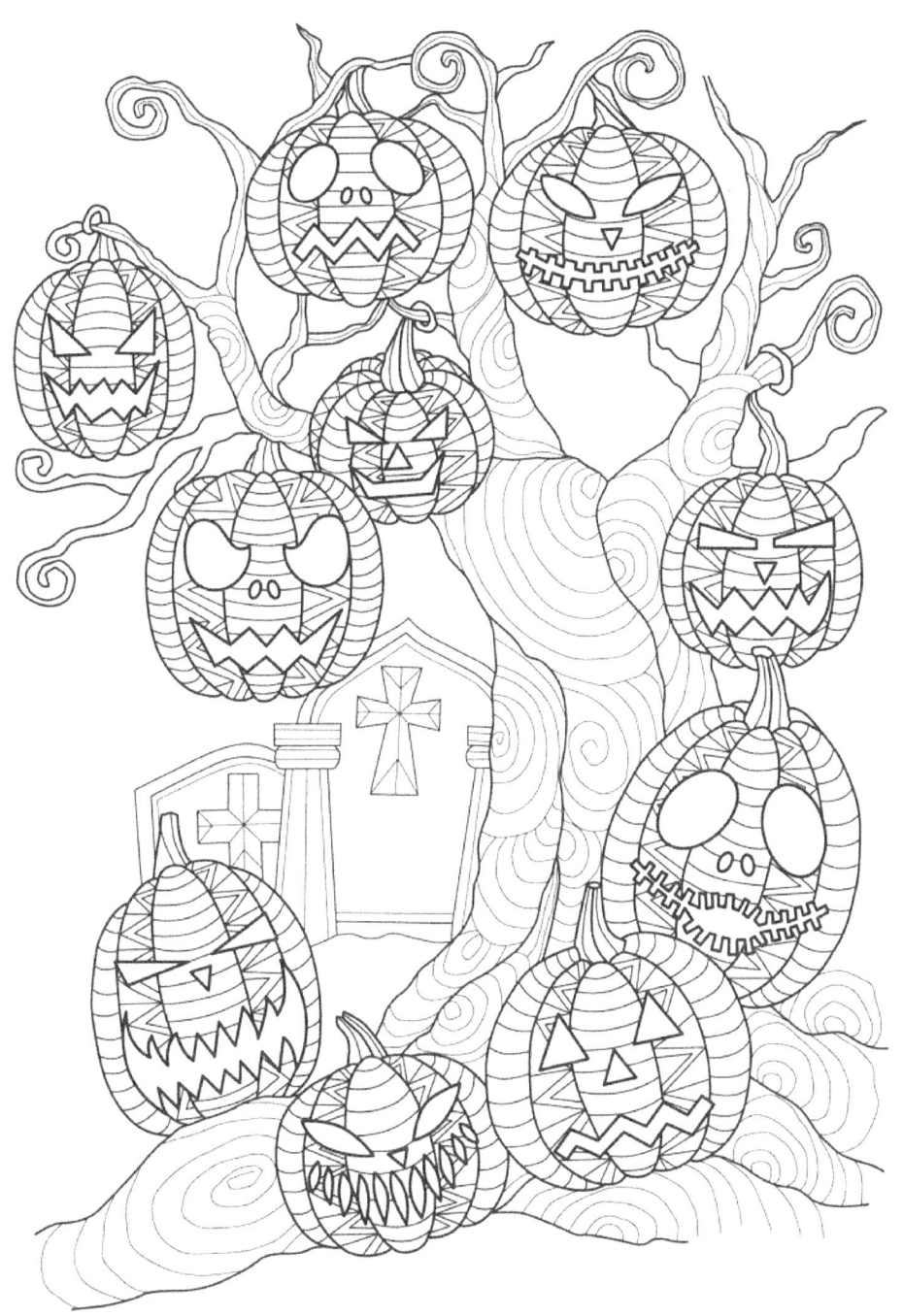

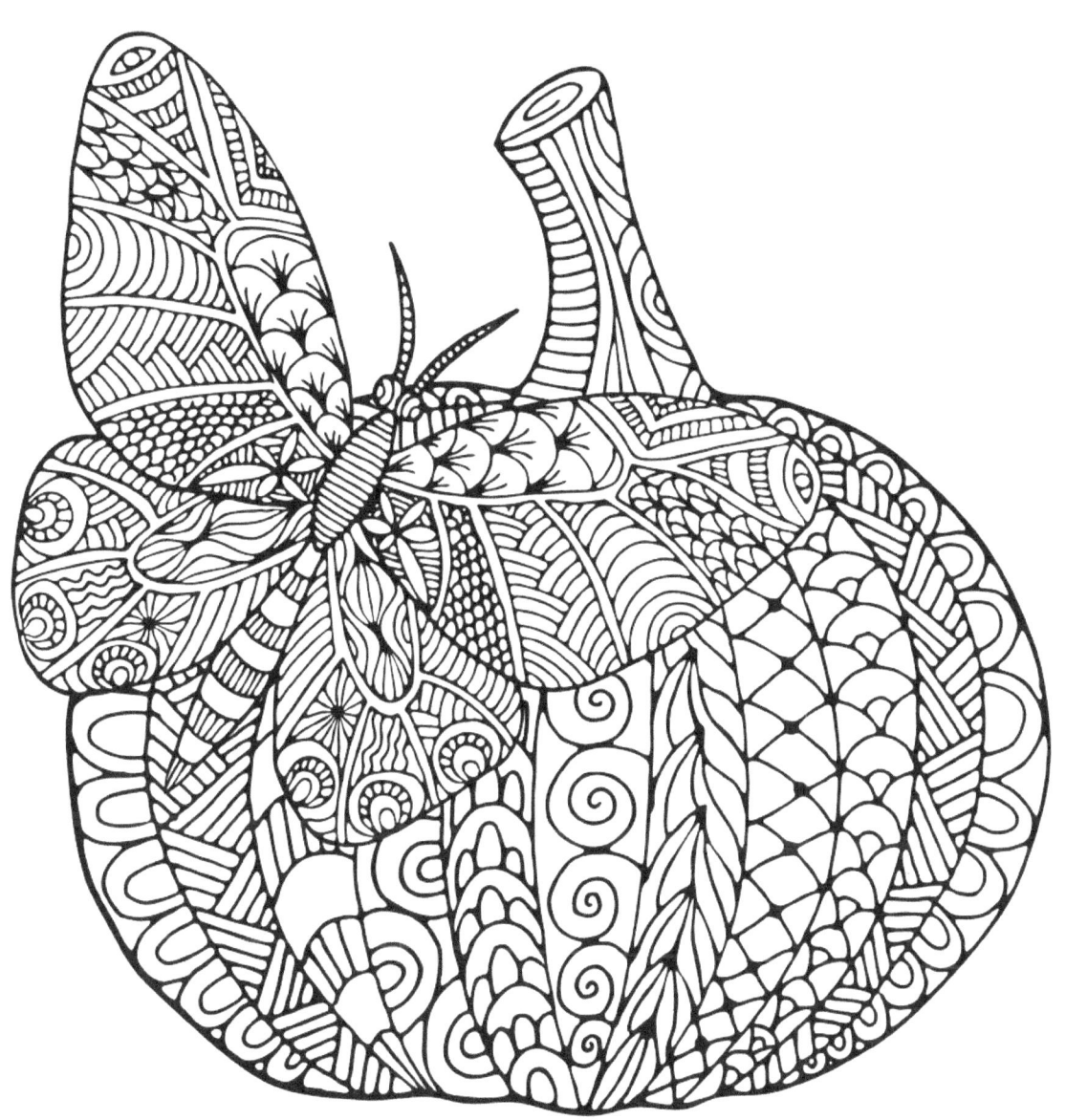

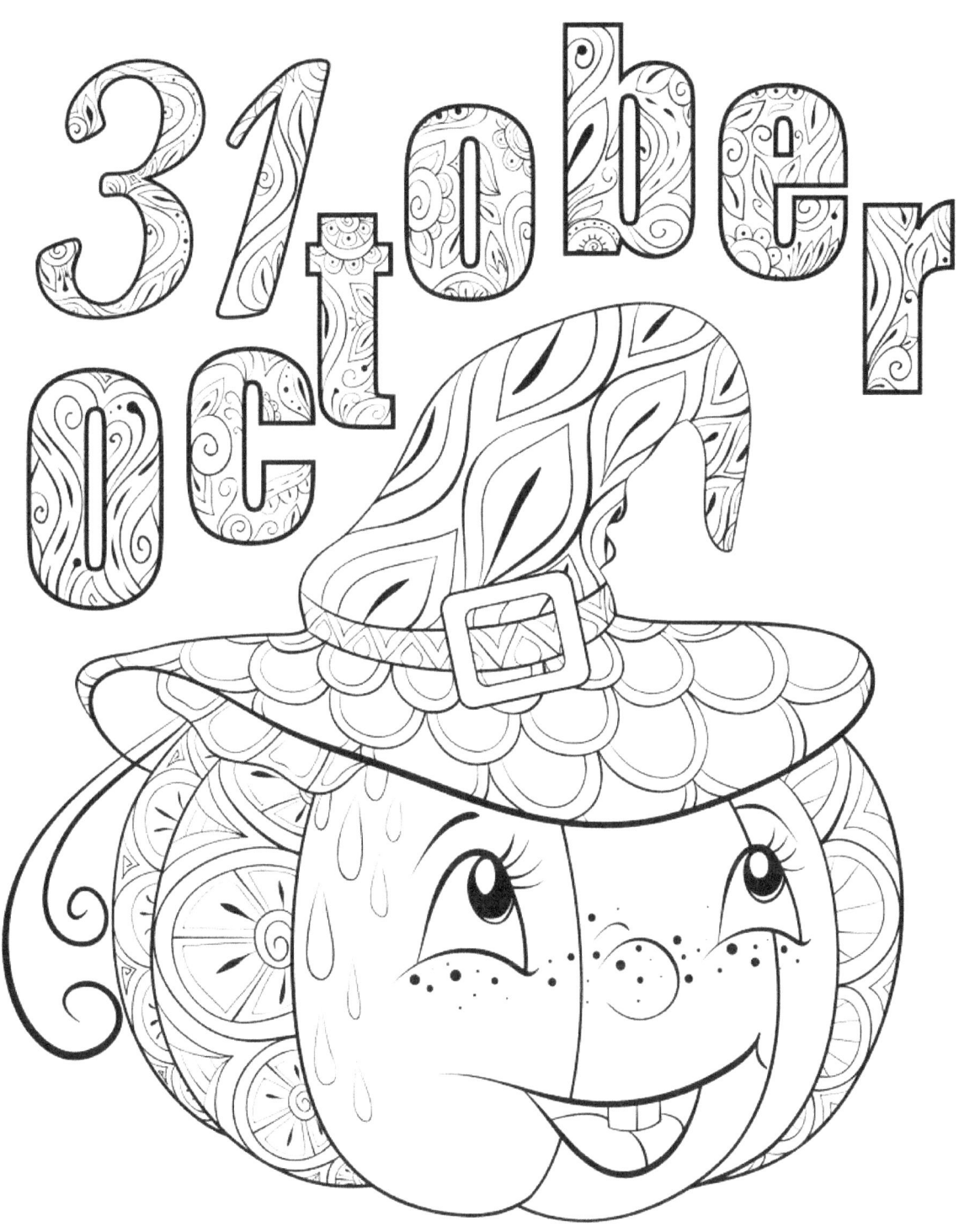

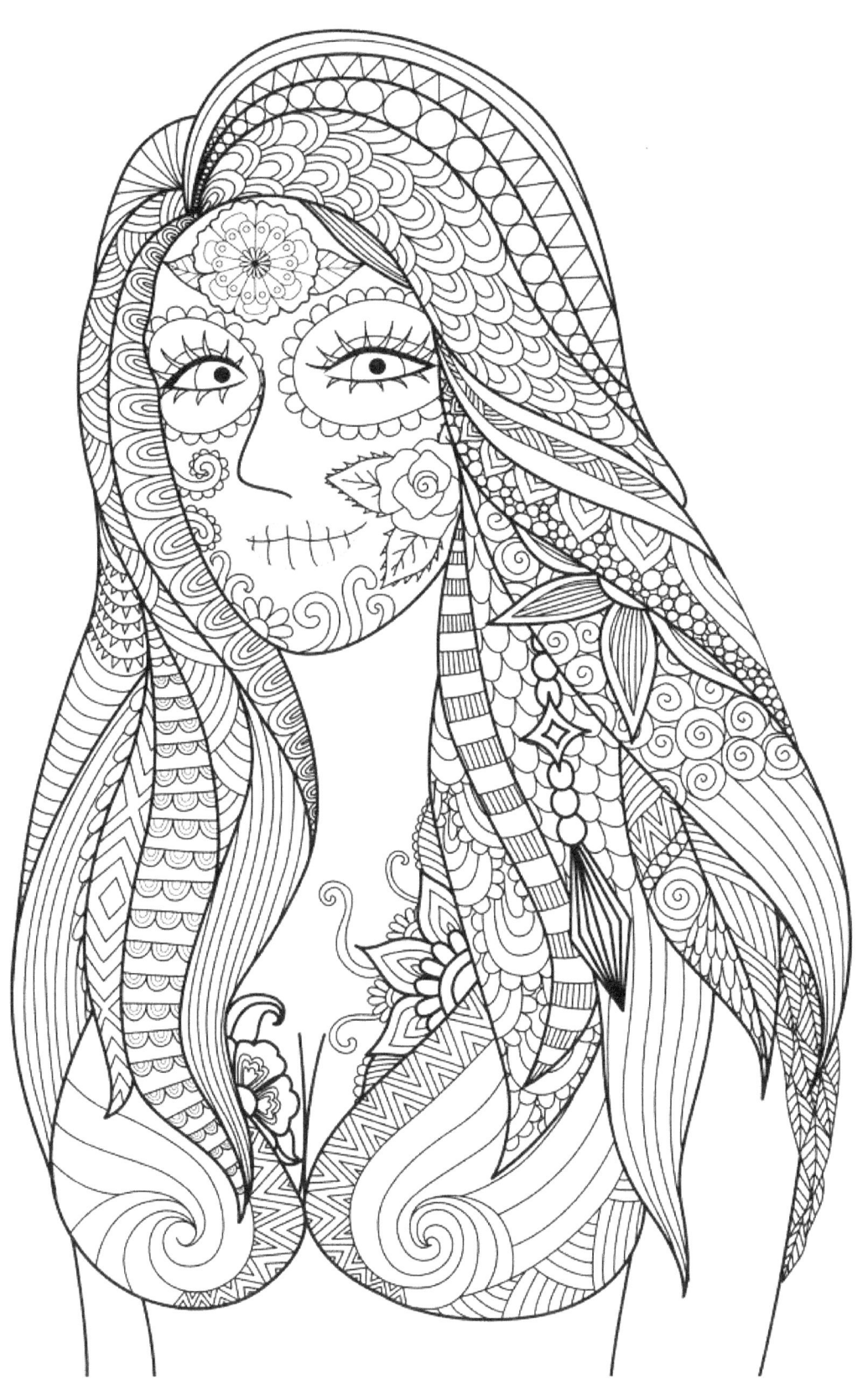

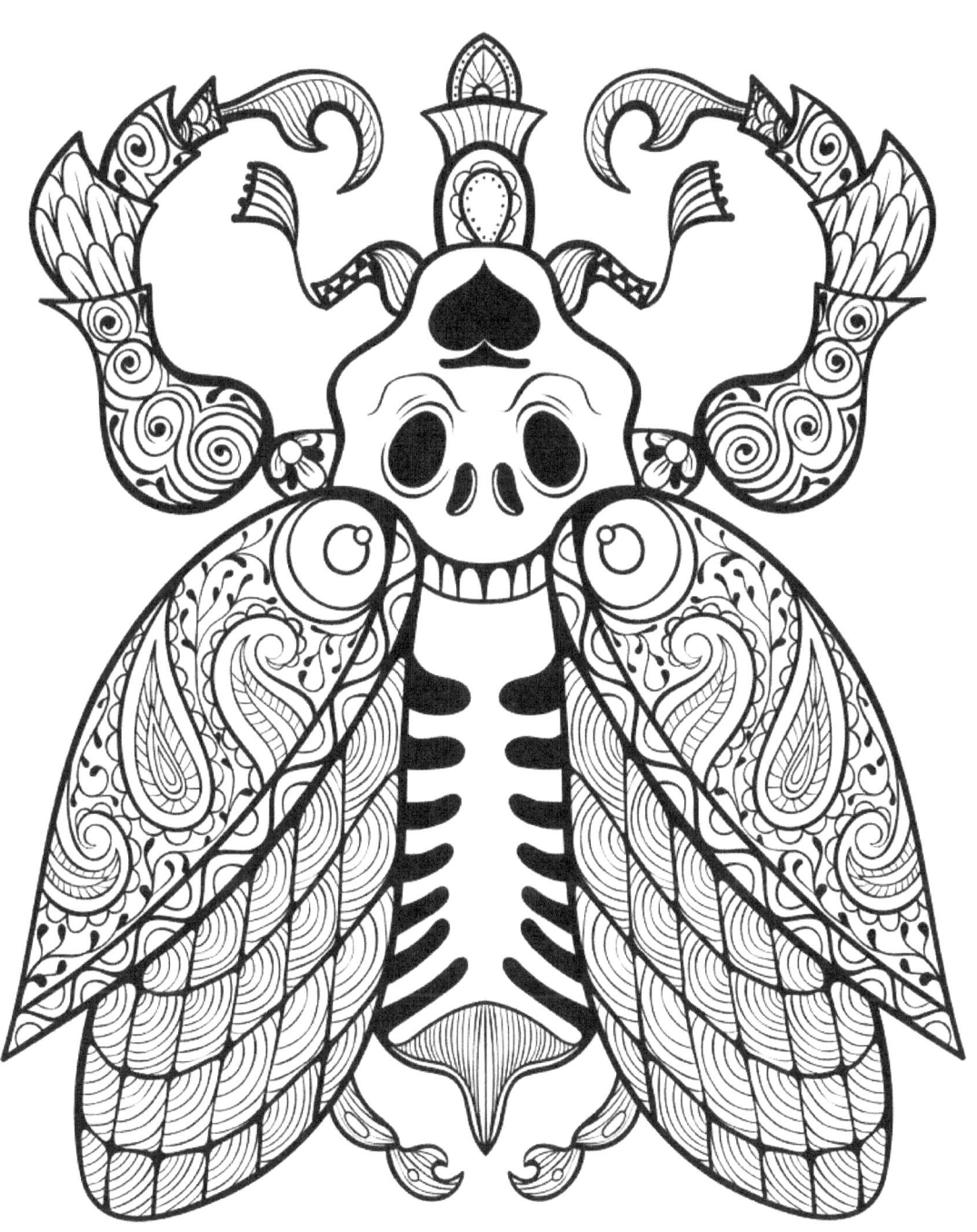

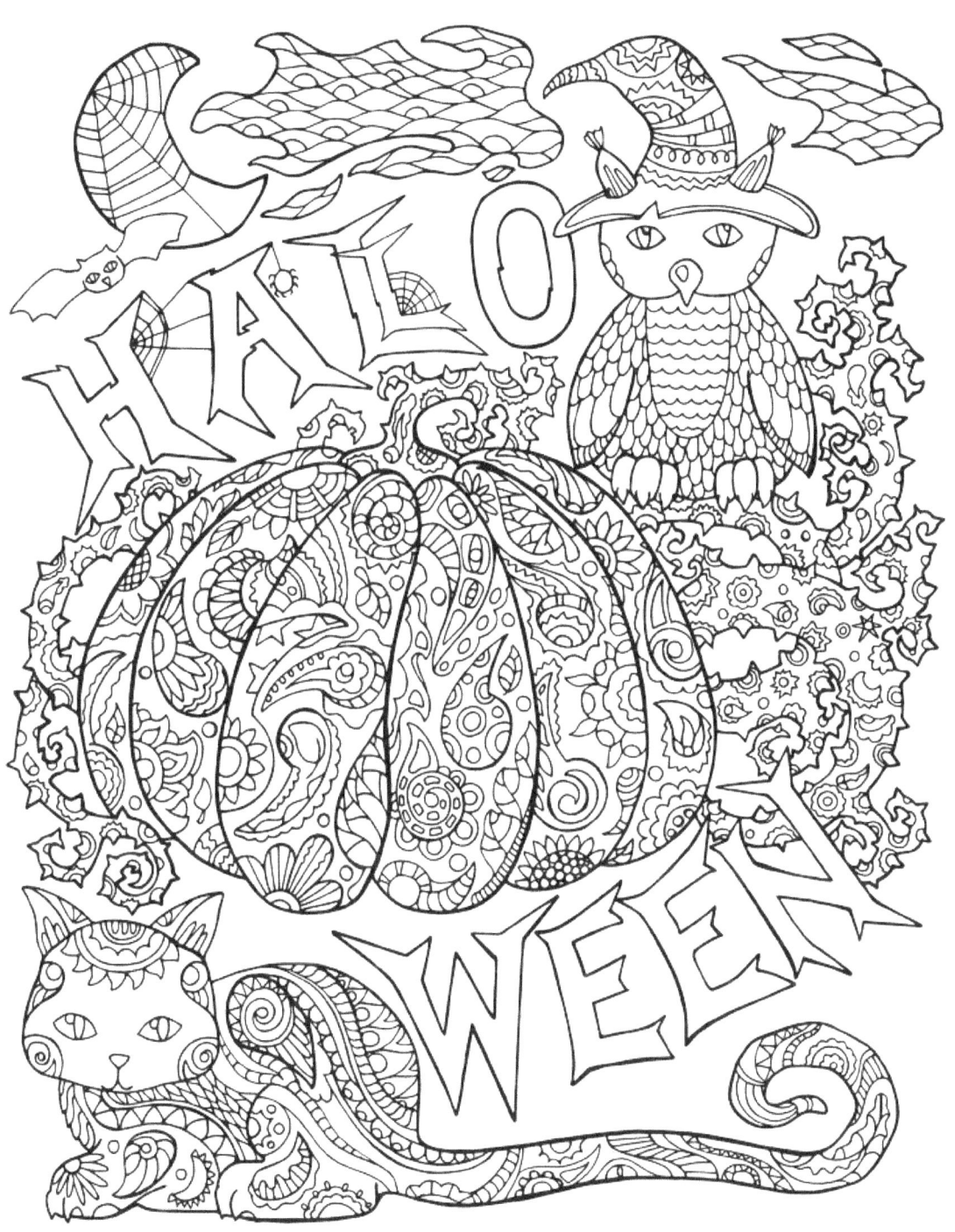

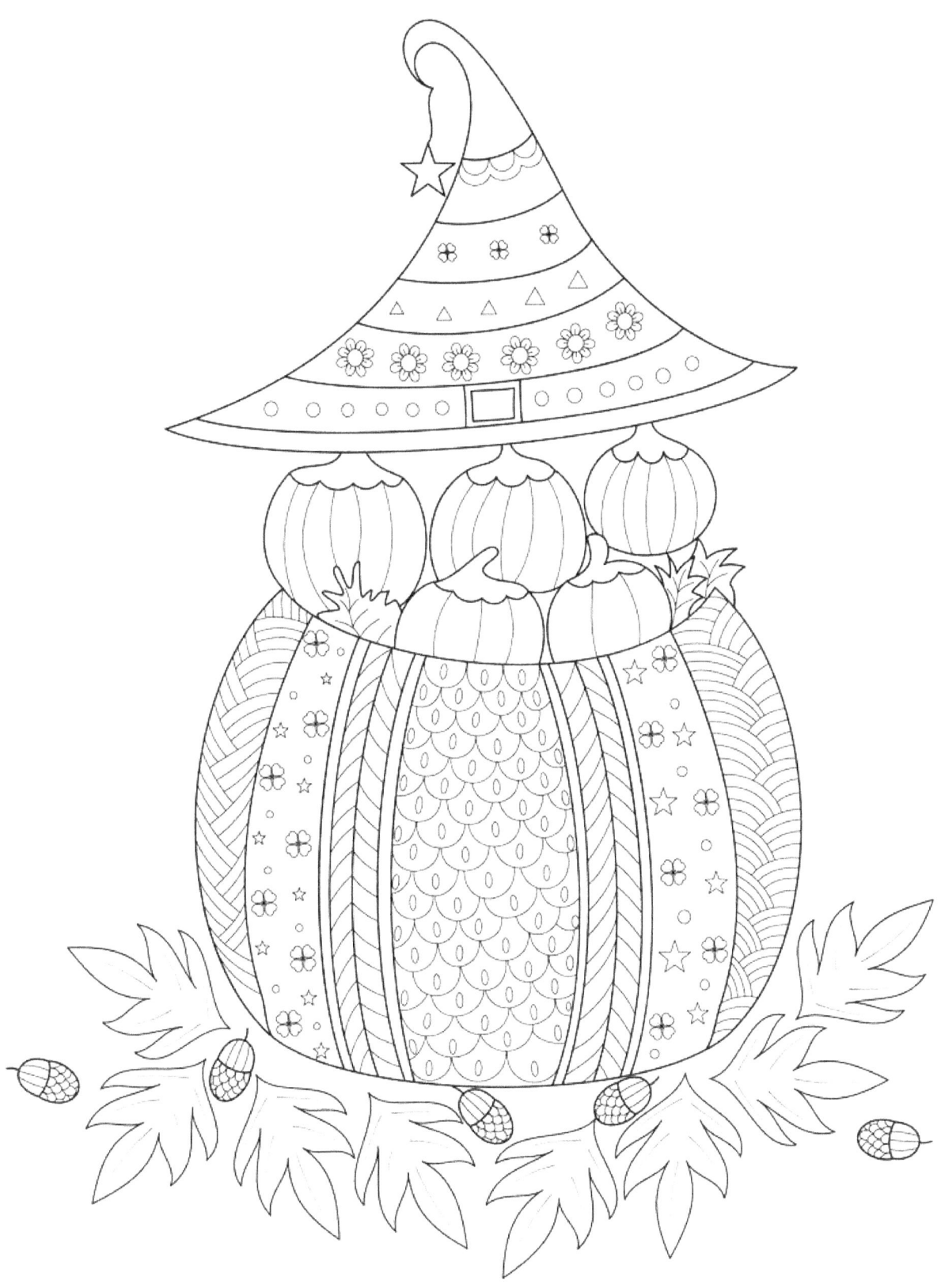

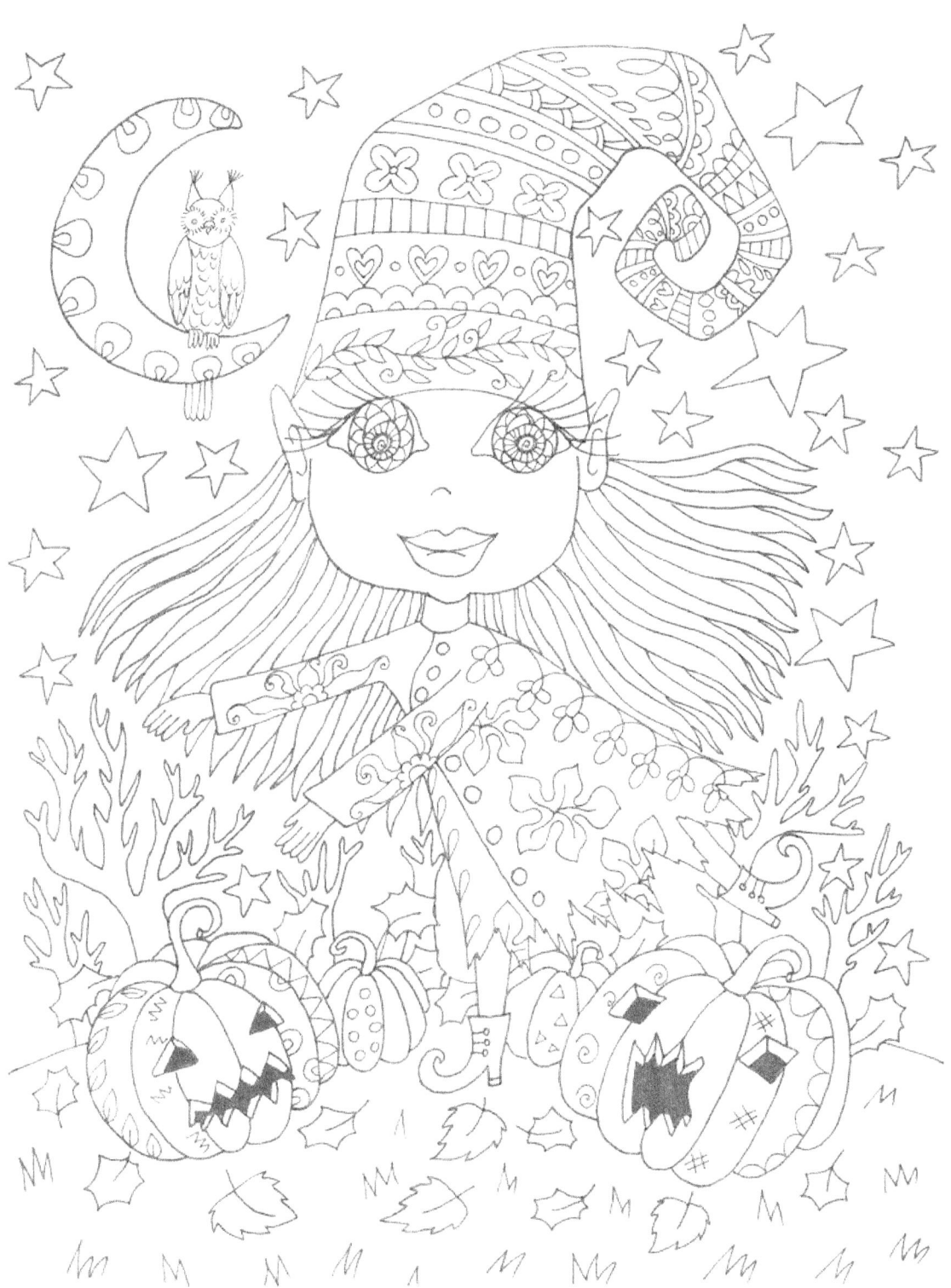

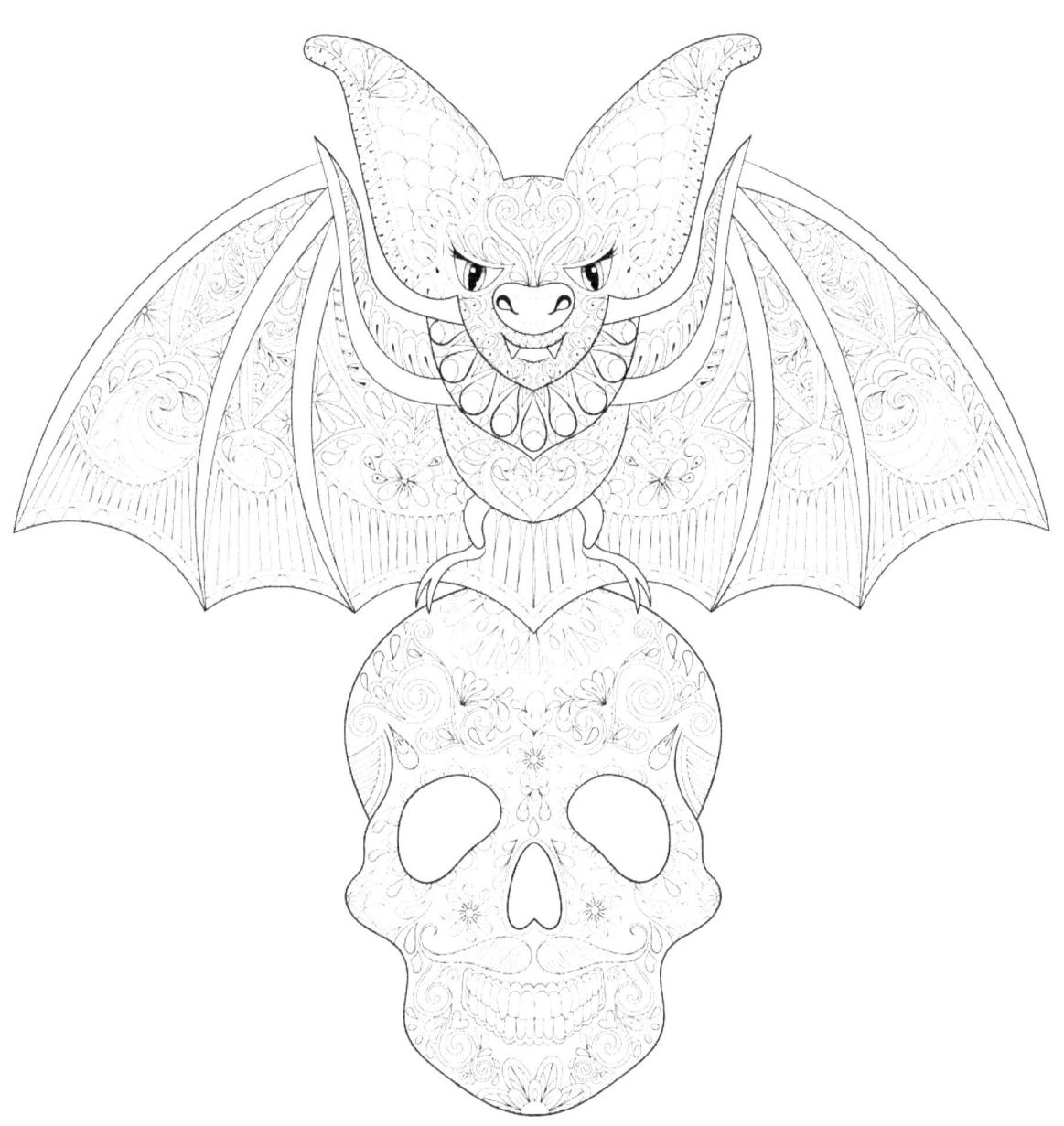

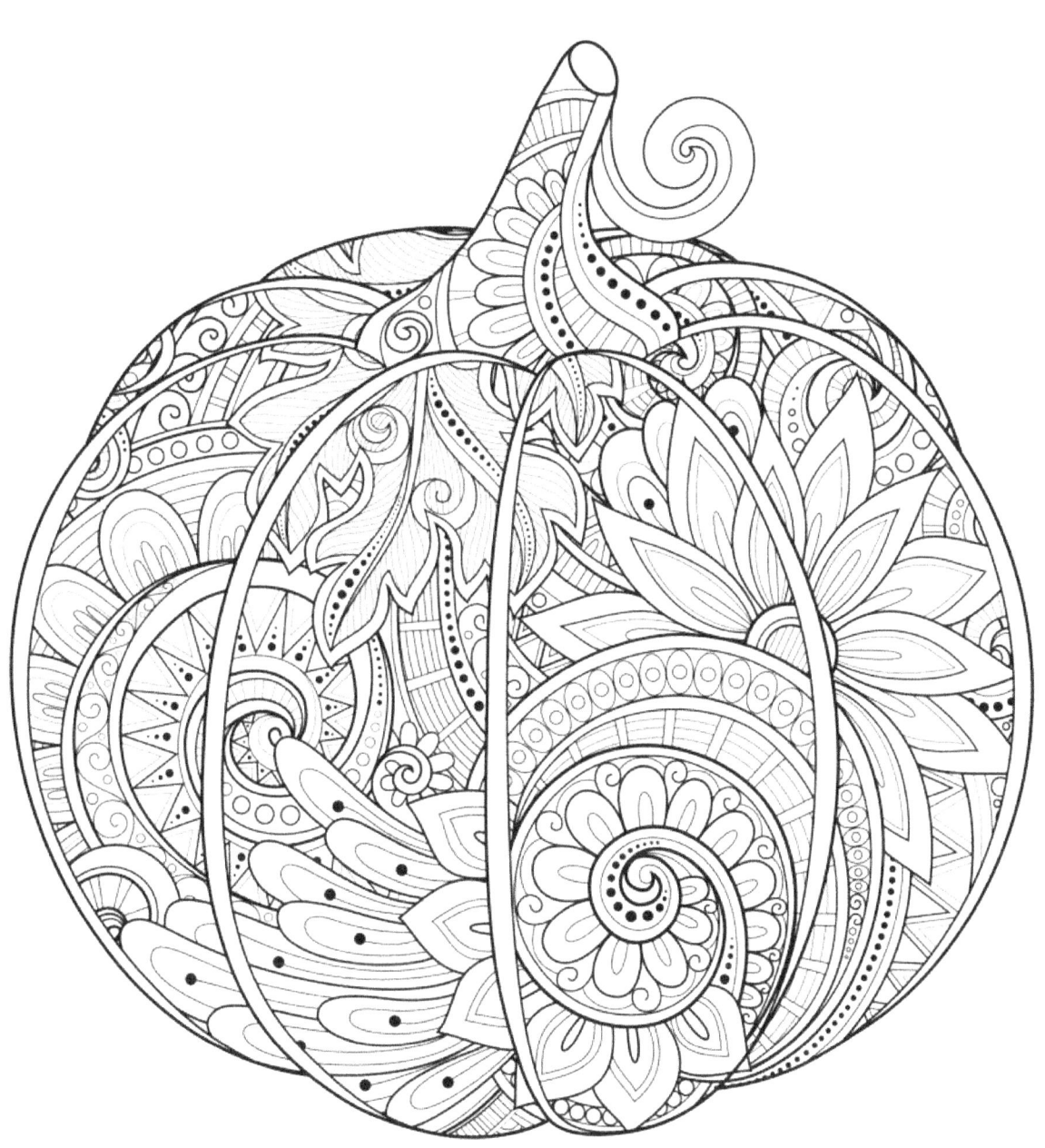

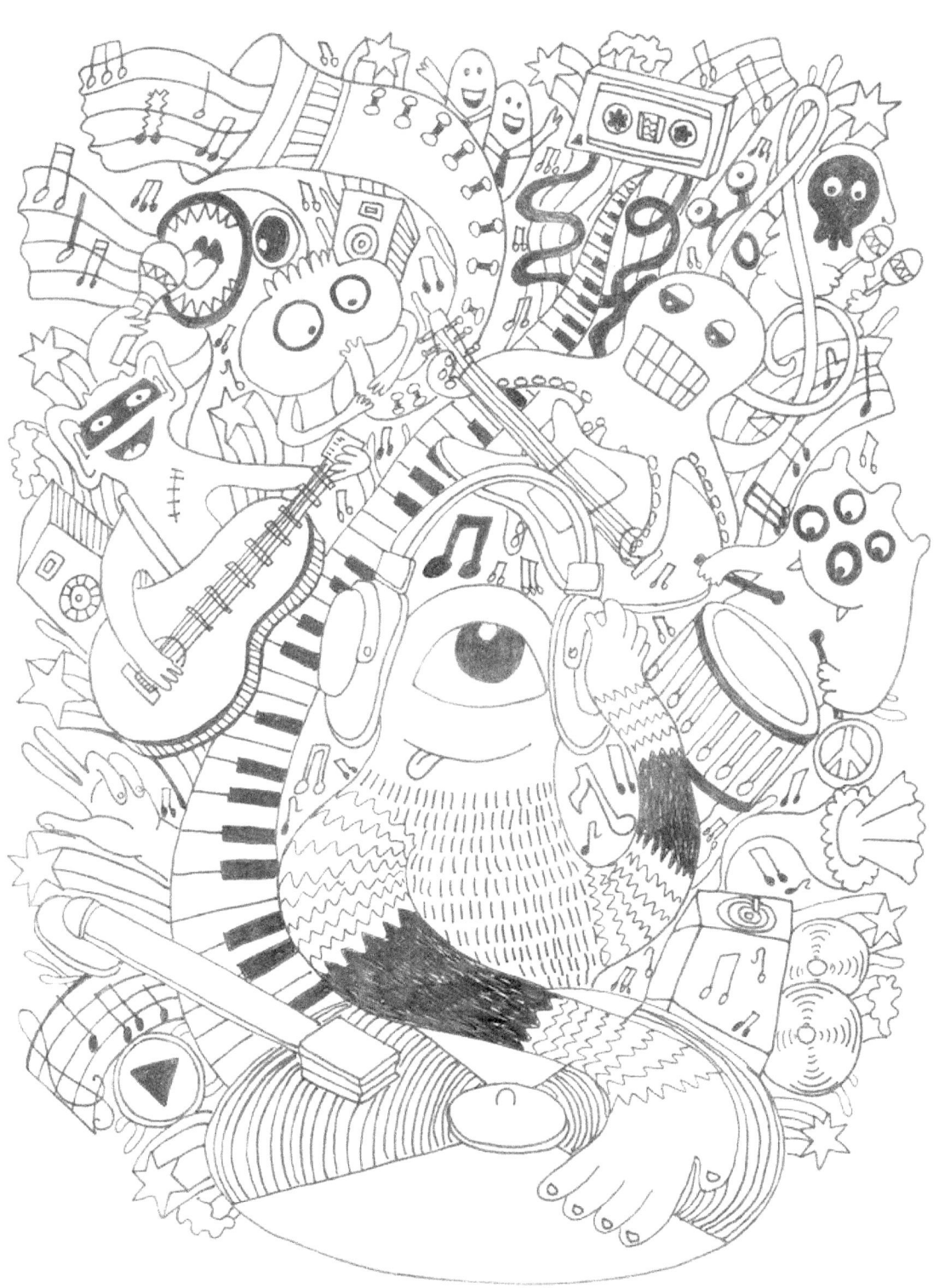

www.ingramcontent.com/pod-product-compliance
Lightning Source LLC
Chambersburg PA
CBHW062341220526
45469CB00008B/2797